Contents

Bellerophon and the Chimera

Bellerophon was the handsome and charming prince of Corinth. His good looks and friendly manner made him very popular in his country, but he was forced to flee his home and live in exile when he accidentally killed an important citizen.

The young prince travelled for many miles, until he reached the court of Proteus, the king of Argos. Taking pity on Bellerophon, the king gave him refuge in his home.

After a while, Bellerophon began to enjoy his new life and made many friends. But his popularity also brought him trouble; for the king's wife, Anteia, fell in love with him. Knowing that if King Proteus discovered his wife's true feelings he would be banished from Argos forever, Bellerophon did his best to avoid the queen. This made Anteia angry and she decided to seek revenge.

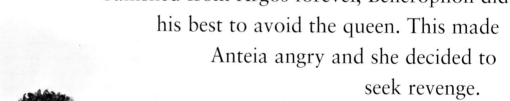

Fantastic Creatures from Greek Myths

Retold by Pat Posner

Illustrated by Olwyn Whelan

B R I M A X

Introduction

Thousands of years ago, the people of ancient Greece worshipped gods and goddesses who had superhuman strengths and powers. They could cover vast distances in the blink of an eye, transform themselves into other creatures, and, of course, they were immortal. But they also had very human faults and flaws, such as jealousy, anger, and greed.

The stories in this book recount the exploits of six courageous heroes and their dealings with these gods and goddesses. Sometimes the gods and goddesses helped the heroes on their missions, but other times they were spiteful and set obstacles in their way. During the course of their adventures, the heroes also encountered a wide range of fantastic creatures, from flying horses and fierce lions, to horrible giants and many-headed monsters.

Stories about heroes and magical creatures, called myths, were told by travelling storytellers, who journeyed all over ancient Greece. There is no one correct version of the myths because these stories evolved over time, as they were passed down orally from generation to generation. Historians learned about these stories by studying artifacts such as ancient vases and temple carvings, which told these stories in pictures.

The myths were a way to help the ancient Greeks understand nature and the events in their lives. For example, when it thundered outside, the ancient Greeks thought that the gods on Mount Olympus were angry. Today we have science to explain the world around us, but the ancient Greeks' stories are still exciting to read. The brave heroes' timeless battles, romances, travels, and daring feats remain thrilling stories for modern readers to enjoy.

"My king, Bellerophon is rude and insults me whenever you are not there," the queen told her husband.

Of course, Anteia was lying, but the king did not know this and grew angry. But Proteus knew that he could not harm a guest in his own home without offending the gods.

So the king thought of a plan to get rid of the prince. He asked Bellerophon to deliver a letter to Anteia's father, Iobates, the King of Lycia. The letter told Iobates that Bellerophon had insulted Anteia and should be put to death, as the honour of his daughter was at stake.

Believing that the sealed letter contained innocent news, Bellerophon set off happily. After a long journey, Bellerophon arrived at Iobates' court, where he was welcomed by the king himself. Pleased to hear news of his daughter, Iobates put the letter from King Proteus aside and forgot all about it for several days.

By the time Iobates read the letter, he had grown to like the prince and he, too, felt that he could not kill a guest without upsetting the gods. Iobates was not sure what to do. Then he remembered the Chimera, a terrifying monster that was half-lion, half-goat, and had the tail of a viper snake.

Calling for Bellerophon, the king said, "My son-in-law tells me in his letter that you are a brave man. There is a terrible monster living not far from here that kills my people and destroys their land. Many men have died trying to slay it. Now, I wonder if you are brave enough to destroy this creature?"

Iobates was sure that the Chimera would kill Bellerophon, as the monster was even more terrifying than he had told the prince. Its lion's head breathed fire and it moved like a mountain goat, twisting and turning to avoid anything aimed at it. Its snake's tail thrashed and slashed through the air, spitting a deadly poison from its long, sharp fangs.

Bellerophon knew that Iobates would think him a coward if he refused, so he accepted the challenge. That night, as Bellerophon slept, the goddess Athena appeared to him.

The beautiful goddess, who felt sorry for the young prince, whispered, "If you have any hope of slaying the Chimera, you must be mounted on the winged wild stallion named Pegasus. No man so far has ever been able to ride the beast." Athena handed Bellerophon a golden bridle. "Take this, for without it you will never tame Pegasus," she said.

The next morning, Bellerophon saw Pegasus. The beast's long, lean body was far more beautiful than that of any ordinary horse, and his huge, white wings carried him gracefully across the sky. As Pegasus drank from a spring, Bellerophon crept closer to the wild beast and threw the golden bridle over its head. The stallion bucked and snorted with anger, but the prince held on tightly. At last, Pegasus calmed down and Bellerophon climbed onto its back.

Flapping his huge wings, Pegasus soared up into the sky, carrying Bellerophon for many miles, until they saw the hideous Chimera far below.

As the monster spat poison from its snake tail and tried to claw them, Pegasus dodged the fire that belched from its lion's mouth. Bellerophon shot arrow after arrow into the creature's side until the Chimera fell to its knees. Then, taking a lead-tipped arrow, Bellerophon shot it into the Chimera's mouth. The flames melted the arrow's lead and choked the monster to death.

Returning home a hero, Bellerophon married King Iobates' second daughter. Success made the prince grow conceited, and when people said he was like a god, he believed them.

"If I am like a god, then I should visit them," he decided. Leaping onto Pegasus's back, Bellerophon ordered the stallion to fly to Mount Olympus, where the gods lived. Zeus, the ruler of the gods, was furious and released an insect, which stung Pegasus. As the horse reared up, Bellerophon fell to the ground.

Zeus smiled as he watched Pegasus fly away – the beautiful beast was free once more. Bellerophon, who was now lame, was left to roam the land, alone and unhappy. Nobody would dare befriend a man who had angered the god of gods!

Perseus and the Gorgon

King Acrisius of Argos had a daughter named Danae, who gave birth to a beautiful baby boy. Most new grandparents are delighted, but not King Acrisius – he was worried. Many months before, he had visited a fortune teller. This wise, old woman had warned him that his daughter would have a child, and that one day the child would kill him.

King Acrisius did not want to die, so he came up with a plan. One very windy night, King Acrisius told his soldiers to bring him a large, wooden chest. When Danae and his baby grandson Perseus were asleep, he put them inside and closed the lid. Then he and the soldiers carried the chest down to the sea and pushed it into the storm-tossed waves.

The king felt safe now. He thought that Perseus and Danae would starve to death inside the chest or, if it burst open, they would drown or be eaten by sea monsters. But none of these things happened.

After days at sea, the chest was washed up on the shores of Seriphos, an island ruled by King Polydectes. The king's brother, Dictys, found the chest and opened it to discover Danae and her son inside. They were tired and hungry after their stormy journey.

Taking pity on them, he said, "You can live with me and my wife in our cottage." Perseus and his mother lived happily on Seriphos for many years, as Perseus grew up into a strong and handsome young man. But their lives were not without problems. When King Polydectes met his brother's guests, he fell in love with Danae. He ordered her to marry him, even though she did not love him.

"I'll do anything to make you change your mind," Perseus begged the king. "Anything!"

The king, who wanted to get Perseus out of the way, thought of a way to get rid of him.

"Find Medusa the Gorgon," he said. "Cut off her head and bring it to me."

Medusa was the most horrid of all Gorgons – tusked creatures with snakes growing out of their heads. Perseus knew that anyone who looked into her eyes was turned into stone, but he set off anyway.

The gods felt sorry for Perseus and admired his bravery, so they decided to help him. Athena, goddess of wisdom and war, gave him a bright, shiny shield.

"Use it as a mirror," she said. "Look in the shield, not at Medusa herself."

The god Hermes gave him a sickle to cut off Medusa's head.

"It's sharp enough to cut through the snakes and bones in Medusa's neck," he said.

Then the gods told Perseus to go to Mount Atlas, where he would find the three Grey Ones, who shared a tooth and one eye.

It was misty and murky on the mountain. Perseus could not see much, but he could hear voices squabbling.

"It's my turn for the tooth. I'm hungry, I want to eat."

"I've got the eye. You'll have to get it before you can see to eat."

Perseus crept closer and, through the fog, he saw the Grey Ones passing an eye and a tooth from hand to hand. He asked them where he could find Medusa.

The Grey Ones cackled and carried on passing the eye and the tooth. Suddenly, Perseus grabbed the cold, slimy eye.

"I won't give you your eye back until you've told me," he said.

"The Nymphs in the ocean will tell you," chanted the Grey Ones.

The Nymphs were overjoyed when Perseus told them that he wanted to find and kill Medusa. To help him, they gave him a magic hat that would make him invisible and a bag to put Medusa's head inside.

"She lives in the Gorgons' Lair," they told him. "Put on these winged sandals. They will fly you there."

Perseus flew over jungles, deserts, sea, and land. When he looked down and saw stone statues of people and animals, he knew that he must be close to the Gorgons' Lair. Holding the sickle in one hand and the shield in the other, Perseus made his way past the statues until he saw the Gorgons reflected in the shield.

The Gorgons' wings fluttered like ghosts, their claws rattled and rasped, and they ground their tusks angrily. Each Gorgon had hissing, writhing snakes growing out of her head, but the snakes sprouting from Medusa's head were the longest. Their forked tongues darted in and out as they coiled around her neck.

Still looking into the shield, Perseus raised the sickle. There was a horrible crunching noise as he cut off Medusa's head. The two other Gorgons shrieked in fury, but Perseus put on the Nymphs' magic hat and became invisible. Then he put Medusa's head into the bag and flew away on his winged sandals.

Weeks later, Perseus arrived back in Seriphos. He went to find his mother, who was in the cottage, crying.

"I must marry King Polydectes in an hour," Danae sobbed. Perseus hurried to the king's palace.

"I've brought what you asked for," he said, pulling Medusa's head out of the bag. The horrified king did not have time to look away and was turned into stone. The next day, Dictys became the new king.

And what happened to King Acrisius? Well, one day, at the famous Greek Games, Perseus was throwing the discus. The wind caught the discus and it hit his grandfather's head, killing him. The fortune teller's words had come true!

The Labours of Heracles

As a baby, Heracles lived with his mother and stepfather. But his real father, Zeus, was the ruler of the sky and king of all the gods, so it was no wonder that Heracles was a big, strong baby. People were always saying, "Isn't he growing fast!"

Now this annoyed Zeus's wife, Hera, and made her jealous. She sent two poisonous snakes to kill her husband's son, but baby Heracles strangled the snakes easily. After that, Hera tried to pretend that Heracles did not exist.

Years passed, and Heracles grew up brave and good. In time, he was married, and his wife had several children. Heracles became famous for using his strength to right wrongs and do mighty deeds.

But this fame made it hard for Hera to continue ignoring Heracles. She could no longer pretend that he did not exist, and started hating him more than ever. In fact, she hated him so much that she put a curse on him.

This curse tricked Heracles into thinking that his wife and children were deadly enemies, so one night, he killed them! That broke the curse and Heracles was broken-hearted when he saw what he had done. He hurried to the temple to seek forgiveness and he was told to offer himself as a slave to his cousin, King Eurystheus. The king, helped by Hera, made a list of labours – twelve difficult tasks for Heracles to carry out. They were sure that Heracles would fail.

First, Heracles had to kill a ferocious lion who stole people from their beds and ate them! The lion's hide was so thick and tough that no weapon could pierce it. But Heracles had a plan.

He went to the lion's lair in the forest and called to the beast. The lion leapt out, its enormous mouth snarling, its long claws swiping, and its tail lashing fiercely. Heracles caught hold of the tail and swung the lion round and round until it was dizzy. Then Heracles strangled the lion and skinned it.

"I'll make a sword with these long, sharp claws," he said. "The skin I'll wear as a cloak. It will bring me good luck."

Heracles needed a lot of good luck for his next task. He was supposed to kill the infamous Hydra. The Hydra was a many-headed swamp monster whose hissing mouths spat out a poisonous spray. If anyone cut off one of the heads, two more grew in its place. As if that were not enough, Hera had sent an enormous crab to lurk in the swamp.

But again Heracles had a plan. He took his friend, Iolas, with him to the swamp. Iolas had a special flaming torch. Brandishing the sword made from the lion's claws and jumping to avoid the giant crab's pinching claws, Heracles cut off the Hydra's biggest head. The wriggling stump instantly began to grow two more heads.

"Touch the stump with your torch, Iolas," he shouted. "Burn the skin so no more heads can grow."

As quickly as they could, Heracles cut off heads and Iolas scorched the stumps. Soon only one horrible head remained. The Hydra was furious and afraid. It opened its last hissing mouth and spewed out a great spray of deadly poison. Just then, Heracles jumped high in the air to avoid the crab's pinching claws. The venomous spray missed him and killed the crab instead! Then Heracles cut off the last head, Iolas burnt the last stump, and the Hydra lay dead.

Next, Heracles had to catch a deer with golden antlers and take it to live in the palace grounds. Then, he had to capture a fierce boar that was killing farm animals. The lion-skin cloak seemed to bring Heracles luck. The boar got stuck in a snowdrift, so Heracles bound it with ropes and delivered it to the king. When the king saw the boar with its huge tusks, he was terrified and hid away until the boar was locked up in a pigsty.

After that, Heracles had to clean the king's stables in a day. They had never been cleaned, even though hundreds of animals had lived in them. Dung was everywhere! Clever Heracles dug trenches to divert water from nearby rivers, which washed the stables clean. Digging the trenches was tiring work and Heracles was exhausted. But there was no time to rest – he still had more tasks to complete!

He destroyed a flock of man-eating birds with a bow and arrows and captured a bull that breathed fire. Without pausing for a break, he stole some horses that fed on human flesh, fetched a girdle from a warrior queen, rescued cattle from a giant, and even collected some golden apples guarded by a fierce dragon.

Finally, he was ready to carry out the last task, the most dangerous of all. Heracles was sent to the Underworld, without weapons, to fetch the dog who guarded the gates. Cerberus was no ordinary guard dog. It had three heads and its tail was a serpent. A mane of snakes slithered and hissed around the dog's three barking, snarling heads. As always, Heracles had a plan. He threw his lucky cloak over the heads, grabbed Cerberus around the middle, then squeezed until the beast was unconscious.

Heracles brought Cerberus to King Eurystheus, who was so afraid that he hid again. Heracles had used his strength and wits to finish every task that the king had set him. For his labours, he earned forgiveness and became one of the mighty gods on Mount Olympus.

Jason and the Argonauts

When Jason was little, he lived in the wilderness with his mother. All children love stories, and the story Jason loved most of all was the one about the day he was born.

"Your Uncle Pelias had stolen your father's crown and was ruling Iolcus," Jason's mother would tell him. "I was scared that Pelias would have you killed because you were the rightful heir, so I pretended that you had died at birth and I brought you here."

"One day I'll go to Iolcus and tell my wicked uncle I want my kingdom," vowed Jason. And when he grew up, that is exactly what he decided to do.

On his way to Iolcus, Jason lost a sandal while he was crossing a river. King Pelias had been warned by an oracle to beware a man wearing one sandal, so when he saw a handsome stranger wearing only one sandal he felt worried.

When Jason told Pelias who he was, the crafty king said, "You can be king when I get too old, so long as you fetch the Golden Fleece back from Colchis. It belongs here and we want it back." The fleece was guarded by a fearsome dragon, but Jason was brave and determined to win his kingdom back.

Jason sent for some adventurers and had a great ship built. He called the ship the Argo, which means swift sailing, and the ship's sailors were nicknamed the Argonauts. On their way to Colchis, the Argonauts visited King Phineus to ask for his advice on the dangers ahead. Phineus promised to help if the Argonauts could get rid of the troublesome Harpies.

"They're starving me to death," complained the king. He led Jason and the Argonauts to a table laid with food and reached for a piece of bread. Just then, the banquet hall was filled with the sound of beating wings and loud, screeching laughter. Jason looked up and saw two huge birds with women's heads swooping down. These hideous creatures snatched up food in their hooked beaks, screeching and swooping until every morsel was gone. When they flew off, the birds left a terrible smell behind them.

Two of the Argonauts, named Calais and Zetes, had wings, as they were the North Wind's sons. They flew after the Harpies, who clawed at them. But Calais and Zetes were strong and they drove the Harpies away.

Phineus kept his promise and told Jason about twin rocks that floated in the sea like iron icebergs. The two rocks would crash together and crush any ship that tried to pass between them.

"I'll give you a dove," said Phineus. "Send it through the rocks first, and it will make them crash shut. As they re-open, row between them quickly before they crash shut again."

Jason and the Argonauts did exactly what Phineus had told them. They released the dove and watched carefully. The bird flew so quickly that the rocks only crushed one of its tail feathers. As the rocks re-opened, Jason shouted at his crew to row faster than they had ever rowed before. When the rocks crashed shut again there was a splintering of wood, but only the stern of the Argo was damaged. The Argonauts were safely through and the land of Colchis lay ahead.

Colchis was ruled by King Aeetes. When they arrived, Jason told Aeetes that he had come to claim the Golden Fleece.

"First," said the king, "you must hitch my two fire-breathing bulls to a plough. Then, plough a field and plant some dragon's teeth." The king smirked to himself. If the bulls did not burn Jason to death, he would surely be killed when he planted the dragon's teeth. But Aeetes would not have smiled had he known that his daughter, Medea, had fallen in love with Jason.

Medea had strange magical powers. She gave Jason a potion to protect him from fire. When he harnessed the bulls and started to plough, their flaming breath touched his body but did not burn him. The field was soon ready for planting. As Jason sprinkled the last handful of dragon's teeth into the earth, an army of fierce giants sprang up from the soil.

Before the giants could attack him, Jason picked up a stone and threw it, hitting one of the giants on the back of his head. The giant spun round and hit the giant behind him. A fight broke out, the rest of the giants joined in, and soon they all lay dead.

Medea led Jason to a wood. Hanging from a branch of a tree was the Golden Fleece. The dragon was coiled around the tree, its snarling mouth and sharp spikes stretched towards them.

Medea began to sing a strange chant. Her magical voice charmed the dragon and it grew sleepy. Slowly, Medea crept nearer and sprinkled sleeping dust on the creature. Once the dragon was snoring, Jason grabbed the Golden Fleece and sailed back to Iolcus with Medea.

For a while, Jason was treated as a hero – but he still wanted to be king. Medea told Pelias's daughters that if they boiled him in a cauldron, he would become young again. This killed Pelias and freed the throne for Jason. But people did not like Medea's trickery and sneaky ways. She and Jason were banished from Iolcus.

They went to Corinth, where Jason became king. There, he fell in love with a princess. In a jealous rage, Medea killed the princess and fled the country. Jason was forced to leave, too. He roamed for years and years, until one day, he came across the Argo's rotting hull. While Jason sat beside the ship, remembering his adventures of long ago, a piece of its timber hit him on the head. The Argo, which once brought him such good fortune, killed him in the end.

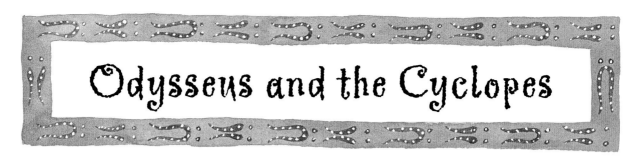

Odysseus and the Cyclopes

The Greeks and the Trojans had been fighting for ten years, but the Greek soldiers could not conquer the city of Troy. That was, until Odysseus, a brave and clever Greek, came up with a cunning plan. He designed a big wooden horse with a trap door in its belly. The horse was wheeled into the gates of Troy as a gift, but dozens of Greek soldiers were hidden inside. When darkness fell, the soldiers crept out of the horse, overpowered the guards and opened the city gates to let in the rest of the army.

A few hours later, the city of Troy was burnt to the ground. The war was over and, before long, the Greek soldiers boarded their ships and set sail for their homes. After sailing for many weeks, Odysseus and his crew were so tired and hungry that they decided to land on the next island they saw. Leaving their ship beneath a cliff, they began to explore.

After climbing to the clifftop, they saw sheep grazing in green, rolling meadows. The island seemed to be a beautiful and peaceful place. Little did Odysseus and his shipmates know that this was the island of the Cyclopes – huge and hideous one-eyed cannibals.

"There must be shepherds to look after the sheep," reasoned Odysseus. "And shepherds have to eat, so there will be food for us on this island!"

Soon, they found a cave with a wide, high entrance. Inside, they saw some massive logs, hollowed out and full of ewe's milk. Stacked at the back of the cave were several enormous cheeses. The hungry soldiers were about to break off some cheese to eat when suddenly they heard the bleating of sheep. Then the ground began to shake and over the noise of the bleating they heard a thunderous thumping sound.

The sheep crowded into the cave and behind them, stooping to get through the high entrance, followed the shepherd. Odysseus and his shipmates gasped and crept to the back of the cave. The shepherd, Polyphemus, was gigantic! Even though his bulk cut out the light from outside, they could see one huge eye, gleaming from the centre of his forehead. Using his huge foot, the giant easily rolled a boulder as big as a house across the cave's entrance. Odysseus knew that all of his men together would not be able to move the rock. They were trapped!

Polyphemus milked his ewes then lit a fire, which lit up the cave's shadows.

"Aha!" bellowed Polyphemus. "I see I've got visitors. How brave of you to come. Are you the heroes I've heard so much about?"

Odysseus stepped forward. "I'm nobody, really," he said modestly. "My – "Odysseus had been about to tell Polyphemus his name, but the giant interrupted him.

"Well, Nobody, I'll enjoy the company of you and your friends less and less every day." Roaring with laughter, Polyphemus reached out one huge arm and snatched up two men. After crushing them in his fist, he popped the men in his vast mouth and gulped them down with one swallow.

The next morning, Polyphemus crushed two more men in his fist, then swallowed them whole. After this breakfast, he moved the boulder and drove the sheep out in front of him.

"I'll see you and your little men later, Nobody," he jeered, pointing at Odysseus. Then he rolled the boulder back to block the cave's entrance.

That night, after he had milked his ewes, lit the fire, and eaten two more men, Polyphemus drank some wine and fell into a deep sleep. Odysseus, who had spent all day working out a daring plan, pulled out a huge wooden stake that he had found at the back of the cave. After heating the point in the fire, he climbed on to Polyphemus's chest and drove the burning stake into the giant's single eye.

"Now you won't be able to see us any more," panted Odysseus.

Polyphemus screamed so loudly that all the other Cyclopes who lived on the island came running.

"Are you all right, Polyphemus?" they called through the boulder.

"I'm blind!" howled Polyphemus.

"Who has blinded you? Who's in there with you?"

Polyphemus, who thought that Odysseus's name was Nobody, answered with an angry roar. "Nobody is here. Nobody has blinded me!" The other Cyclopes, assuming that Polyphemus had just had a nightmare, went back to their own caves.

When the sheep started bleating in the morning, Polyphemus felt his way along the walls of the cave until he reached the boulder. The blinded giant rolled it back just enough for one sheep at a time to go out.

"Don't think you and your men can get out, Nobody," he said. "I can't see, but I can feel." Polyphemus felt each sheep's back as it went out to make sure no human was sitting on it.

"You didn't feel underneath the sheep," shouted Odysseus, from outside the cave. He had instructed his men to cling to the sheep's bellies. "And my name isn't Nobody, my name is Odysseus. You will never forget it because you will hear much more about the great deeds my men and I will do!"

Odysseus was right. They had many more adventures before they finally arrived home.

Theseus and the Minotaur

As a young boy, Theseus knew that his father was King Aegus, even though he had never met him. He was very curious about the king.

"When will I get to meet my father?" he was always asking his mother. She would take him to an enormous rock and tell him that, under the great stone, his father had left him a special sword and a pair of golden sandals.

"When you are strong enough to lift this rock, you can go to meet your father," she would say.

At last the day came when Theseus could budge the rock. He heaved with all his might, until finally, the rock came out of the earth. He put on the sandals, picked up the sword, and prepared to travel to his father's palace in Athens.

"Your grandfather says to go by sea because there are many dangers on the road," warned Theseus's mother. But brave, young Theseus wanted adventure, so he decided to walk to Athens.

Theseus's grandfather was right; there was no shortage of danger along his route. Shortly after he set off, a giant threatened to pound him to death. Quick-thinking Theseus grabbed the giant's club and killed him instead, then carried on his way. This was not the last fearsome creature he encountered. Further along the way, a fierce wild sow blocked his path, snorting and pawing the earth, but Theseus slew it with his father's sword.

Theseus had nearly reached Athens when a giant called Sciron challenged him on the cliff path.

"Wash my feet," roared Sciron. "Then I'll kick you into the sea as a feast for my tortoise."

Theseus knelt down, as if he were about to obey the giant's order. He quickly grabbed Sciron's ankles and pulled with all his strength. Sciron thudded to the ground. With a mighty shove, Theseus rolled him over the cliff, into to the enormous tortoise's open mouth. Then he carried on his way to Athens.

Theseus was cheered when he arrived in Athens, for the city's people had heard of his brave deeds. When King Aegeus saw the golden sandals and the sword, he recognized this hero as his son.

Medea, the king's second wife, was jealous. Now Theseus, and not her son, would be heir to the throne. She resolved to get rid of this newcomer and poured him some poisoned wine.

But when Theseus saw the sly look in her eyes he said, "You drink from it first." Howling with rage, Medea flung the glass to the floor. Then she called for her chariot and rode away from Athens forever.

Theseus soon settled into his new life in Athens. After so many years wondering about his father, he enjoyed getting to know the king. One morning, from outside the palace, came the sound of people wailing.

"Father, why are your people so sad?" asked Theseus.

Sighing, King Aegeus answered sadly, "King Minos of Crete has sent his messenger to fetch seven youths and seven maidens. If we do not send them, King Minos will wage war against us."

Then his father told him about the Minotaur, a horrible monster – half man and half bull - that fed upon human flesh. Every nine year's, to satisfy a war debt to Crete, fourteen young Athenians were taken to a dreadful labyrinth. There they would wander the dark passages until the Minotaur found them and ate them.

"I will be one of the men," volunteered Theseus courageously. "I will go to Crete and kill the Minotaur."

King Aegeus pleaded with his son to change his mind, but Theseus would not be swayed.

"All right," agreed the king. "You'll travel on a ship with a black sail. If you survive, raise a white sail on your return and I'll know you are alive."

So Theseus, his sword hidden inside his tunic, boarded the ship. When he landed on the island, Theseus and the others were stripped of their weapons and taken to the dungeon.

King Minos's daughter, Ariadne, had watched the prisoners arrive and had fallen instantly in love with Theseus. Late that night, she crept into the dungeon.

"Theseus," she whispered, "if I help you, will you take me to Athens and marry me?" Theseus promised and Ariadne gave him back his sword and some string.

In the morning, the guards pushed the fourteen young people into the labyrinth. Theseus tied one end of the string to the entrance and told the others to wait there. Some of the dark and dreary passages led nowhere. Others took Theseus deeper inside. As he moved closer to the labyrinth's centre, Theseus could hear the blood-curdling roar of the hungry Minotaur.

Suddenly, he came face-to-face with the hideous monster. Theseus gave a blood-curdling roar of his own and drove his sword through the monster's heart. Once the dying monster had crumpled to the ground, Theseus followed the string back to the entrance. The Athenians ran cheering to the ship where Ariadne was waiting. But Theseus did not keep his word. When they stopped at an island a few days later, he left Ariadne there and sailed on towards Athens.

Back in Athens, King Aegeus was watching for the ship. But once again, Theseus did not keep his word. He had forgotten to change the sail from black to white. When the king saw the black sail, he thought it meant his son was dead. Distraught, King Aegeus threw himself into the sea and drowned.

If only Theseus had kept his word, his father would be alive. So when he became king, grief-stricken Theseus declared that the sea was to be renamed the Aegean Sea, in memory of his father.

Glossary

Anteia	The wife of King Proteus, who fell in love with Bellerophon.
Argo	Jason's ship. His crew were called the Argonauts.
Athena	The Greek goddess of wisdom and war.
Ariadne	The king of Crete's daughter, who fell in love with Theseus.
Bellerophon	A hero and the prince of Corinth.
Calais	A winged Argonaut and the North Wind's son.
Cerberus	A three-headed dog, guardian of the gates to the Underworld.
Chariot	A two-wheeled, horse-drawn vehicle.
Chimera	A terrifying monster, half lion and half goat, with the tail of a snake.
Citizen	A person who lives legally in a particular city or state.
Curse	A spoken spell which asks magical forces to cause the victim harm.
Cyclopes	Giant cannibals with only one eye.
Danae	The mother of Perseus.
Discus	A heavy disc thrown by Greek athletes.
Ewe	A female sheep.
Exile	When someone is banned from their native country.
Girdle	A belt worn around the waist by ancient Greek women.
Gorgon	A horrible creature with snakes growing out of its head.
Harpy	A monster with the head of a woman and the body of a bird of prey.
Hera	Greek goddess; Zeus's first wife.
Heracles	A hero and the son of Zeus.
Hermes	The messenger of the gods.

Hydra	A many-headed swamp monster.
Iobates	The king of Lycia and Anteia's father.
Iolas	Heracles' best friend.
Jason	A hero and the rightful king of Iolcus.
Labour	Hard work.
Labyrinth	A complicated maze.
Lair	A hidden place where animals live.
Medea	A sorceress, who helped Jason find the Golden Fleece and later married King Aegeus.
Medusa	The most fearsome Gorgon of all, who could turn people to stone by looking at them.
Minotaur	A flesh-eating monster, half man and half bull.
Mount Olympus	The home of the Greek gods and goddesses.
Nymph	A female nature spirit.
Odysseus	A Greek soldier and hero of the Trojan war.
Oracle	A place where advice or prophesy was given by priests.
Pegasus	A winged stallion.
Perseus	Grandson of King Acrisius and the slayer of Medusa.
Polyphemus	An enormous Cyclopes, who was slain by Odysseus.
Proteus	The king of Argos.
Sciron	A giant.
Sickle	A short-handled farming tool with a semicircular blade.
Slave	A person who is owned by another person.
Stern	The back part of a ship.
The Grey Ones	Three hags who shared an eye and a tooth between them.
Theseus	A hero and the son of King Aegeus.
Troy	A city state and the deadly enemy of ancient Greece.
Underworld	The place where ancient Greeks believed the dead went.
Zetes	A winged Argonaut and the North Wind's son.